# James Harden

By Jon M. Fishman

AMAZING ATHLETES

Lerner Publications

D0752023

Lerner Publications Company
A division of Lerner Publishing Group, Inc.
241 First Avenue North
Minneapolis, MN 55401 USA

For reading levels and more information, look up this title at www.lernerbooks.com.

Library of Congress Cataloging-in-Publication Data

Fishman, Jon M.
    James Harden / by Jon M. Fishman.
       pages cm. — (Amazing Athletes)
    Includes index.
    Includes webography.
    Audience: Age: 7–11.
    Audience: Grade: K to Grade 3.
       ISBN 978-1-4677-7922-7 (lb : alk. paper) — ISBN 978-1-4677-8113-8 (pb : alk. paper) —
    ISBN 978-1-4677-8546-4 (eb pdf)
       1. Harden, James Edward, 1989– Juvenile literature. 2. Basketball players—United States—
    Biography—Juvenile literature. 3. Oklahoma City Thunder (Basketball team)—History—Juvenile
    literature. 4. Houston Rockets (Basketball team)—Juvenile literature.    I. Title.
    GV884.H2435F57 2016
    796.323092—dc23 [B]                                                    2015013877

Manufactured in the United States of America
1 – BP – 7/15/15

# TABLE OF CONTENTS

James Harden shows off his skills during the 2015 NBA All-Star Game.

# ALL-STAR SUPERSTAR

Houston Rockets **guard** James Harden bounced the basketball and stepped forward. Then he quickly reversed and stepped back. He rose above the court and launched a **three-point shot**. *Swish!*

James was playing for the **Western Conference** in the 2015 NBA All-Star Game. NBA fans had voted for some of the league's biggest stars to play in the game. James received more than one million votes. He didn't waste any time putting on a show for his fans. His three-point shot was the first score for his team. Then he made another three-pointer a few seconds later.

James takes it to the hoop for the Western Conference.

James made an **assist** on his team's next score. Then he sank a **layup** and added another assist. He had scored or assisted all of his team's first 12 points!

Both teams sank shot after shot. The All-Star Game is meant to be a fun show for fans.

The All-Star Game brought out big names such as former president Bill Clinton *(right)* and former NBA player Dikembe Mutombo.

Teams focus on scoring rather than preventing the other team from scoring. James and his teammates took wild shots. They threw fancy passes and high-flying **alley-oops**. By halftime, the West led the **Eastern Conference**, 83–82.

James scores over Pau Gasol of the Eastern Conference.

The action didn't slow down in the second half. James and his teammates were on fire. The West won the game, 163–158. It was the highest-scoring All-Star Game ever!

In 2012, James played for Team USA at the Olympic Games in London, England. He and his teammates won the men's basketball gold medal.

James finished the game with 29 points, 8 **rebounds**, and 8 assists. Houston fans weren't surprised that James had put on such a show. He had the second-best scoring average in the NBA at the time. James had stood out on a team full of superstars at the All-Star Game. "I think I played pretty well," he said. "I just got some shots to fall."

Los Angeles, California, is home to more than three million people.

# LONG SHOT

James Edward Harden Jr. was born on August 26, 1989, in Los Angeles, California. His mother's name is Monja. James's father, James Sr., didn't spend much time with the family. Monja mostly raised James on her own.

James's family lived with crime and violence in the Compton area of South Los Angeles.

James and Monja lived in a dangerous part of Los Angeles. Monja had lost two brothers to violence in the area. She wanted to make sure the same thing didn't happen to James. When James grew old enough to walk around the neighborhood on his own, Monja moved the family to a safer area of the city.

James's new home was in a quieter neighborhood. James had a basketball hoop on wheels that he would push into the street to practice shooting. The area was so quiet that the neighbors sometimes complained when James shot baskets.

Complaining neighbors didn't stop him from practicing. James loved playing basketball. He especially loved sinking long shots. He dreamed about playing in the NBA someday, but his mother wasn't so sure. Monja wanted James to focus on something besides basketball. She thought he should plan for another **career** in case basketball didn't work out.

Monja also worried about James's **asthma**. The problem sometimes made it hard for him to breathe. Monja was concerned about her son running up and down the court during games. But James loved the sport so much that his mother agreed to let him play.

Akili Roberson is James's half brother. He is fourteen years older than James and played football at the University of Kansas.

In 2003, James started as a freshman at Artesia High School. The school often has one of the best high school basketball teams in the Los Angeles area. Former NBA players such as Jason Kapono had gone to school there. It was the perfect place for James to chase his NBA dream while he earned his high school **diploma**.

Former Los Angeles Lakers player Jason Kapono looks to pass during a game against Minnesota in 2012. Kapono attended Artesia High School in the 1990s.

James improved his skills at the Reebok ABCD camp in 2005. High school players go to camps such as this to improve their game before college.

# DRIVING FOR HAMBURGERS

During his first year at Artesia, James didn't look like a future NBA player. He was out of shape and didn't give much effort on the court. James liked to stand away from the basket and take long shots.

"I just stood in the corner [of the court],"
James said. "I didn't **dribble**. I didn't move. I
didn't do anything. I was lazy, really lazy."

He may have been lazy, but he shot the ball
well. Artesia **varsity** basketball coach Scott
Pera thought James had a chance to be a good
player. Pera put James on the school's top team.
He was the only freshman to make the varsity
squad that year.

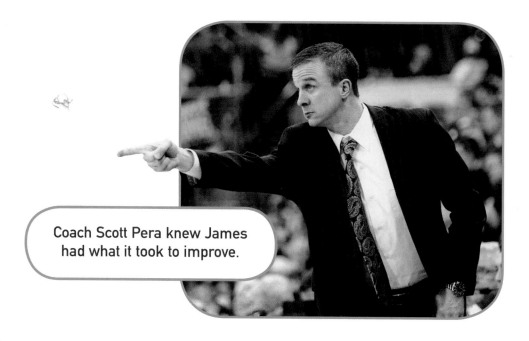

Coach Scott Pera knew James
had what it took to improve.

James's new teammates were all older than him. They convinced him to get in shape and try harder during games. "The older guys straightened him out," Coach Pera said.

James had a new attitude about

James had a long way to go to get in shape for his high school games.

basketball, and he improved on the court. As a sophomore in 2004–2005, he totaled 13.2 points per game for the season. He also averaged 6.4 rebounds, 3.1 assists, and 2.4 **steals**. Artesia won 28 games and lost only five.

Coach Pera wanted James to stop taking long shots so often. Instead, the coach wanted James to **drive** to the basket. Driving to the basket would make the other team more likely to **foul** him in an attempt to slow him down. This would allow him to shoot lots of **free throws**. Free throws are easy points for a good shooter like James.

James *(left)* drives to the basket in a practice game. He would later use this skill to score points in real games.

He made an agreement with his coach. If James shot more than six free throw attempts in a game, Coach Pera would buy him a hamburger. If James shot fewer than six free throws, he would owe his coach a hamburger.

James came into his own in high school as a skilled shooter who wasn't afraid to drive to the basket.

## NATIONAL ATTENTION

By his junior year in 2005–2006, James looked more like a future NBA player. He had grown six inches since his freshman season and now stood six feet six. He was also stronger and in better shape.

The year before, James had attempted 53 free throws. In the 2005–2006 season, after working on driving to the basket with Coach Pera, James attempted 92 free throws. He scored 18.8 points per game and also improved in rebounds, assists, and steals. Even better, Artesia won the state championship!

James sets up to take a free throw. His practice with Coach Pera was paying off.

James looks to pass while playing for Pump-N-Run Elite.

The Amateur Athletic Union (AAU) organizes basketball games for some of the best high school players in the United States. In 2006, James joined an AAU team called Pump-N-Run Elite. They played against teams with future NBA stars such as Kevin Love. James was the scoring star of his team. He sank long shots and stormed to the

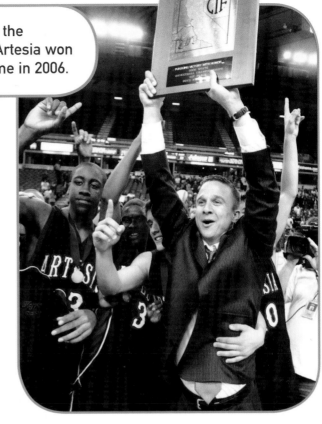

Coach Pera holds up the championship plaque after Artesia won the state championship game in 2006.

basket. He scored 34 points in one game and then put up 33 points in the next game.

James got a lot of attention from college **scouts** after playing with Pump-N-Run. In August 2006, he announced his plan to go to Arizona State University (ASU) after high school. Coach Pera had decided to take a job at ASU. Artesia teammate Derek Glasser had also chosen the school. "I guess it was meant to be for me to come to ASU," James said.

Before going to college, James had one more season to play at Artesia. He scored more than 18 points per game and shot an incredible 238 free throw attempts.

His training with Coach Pera had paid off in a big way. And for the second season in a row, James and his teammates became state champions.

In February 2015, ASU retired James's jersey. That means no ASU player will be able to wear his jersey number (13) in the future.

James's college team didn't have as much success. In 2007–2008, the Arizona State Sun Devils lost 13 games. They finished fifth in their conference. But it was a good first season for James. He shot 224 free throw attempts, second most in the conference. He finished the next season

James drives around Nebraska's Cookie Miller while playing for the Arizona Sun Devils in 2007.

with the most free throw attempts in the conference and scored more than 20 points per game. The Sun Devils ended the year in fourth place.

James talks to reporters after being selected by the Oklahoma City Thunder in the NBA draft.

## TAKING OFF

After his sophomore season at ASU, James decided to move on to the NBA. On June 25, 2009, the Oklahoma City Thunder chose him as the third overall pick in the NBA **draft**. Being chosen so early in the draft put pressure on James. Fans and teammates would expect him to play like a star right away. He wasn't worried. "I don't think I need to prove anything," James said. "I just need to go in there and work hard and try my best to earn a spot on that team."

James worked hard to live up to the hype surrounding him.

Oklahoma City players Russell Westbrook *(left)* and Kevin Durant celebrate a score against the Chicago Bulls.

James earned a spot on the team, but he started most games on the bench during his first few seasons. **Forward** Kevin Durant and guard Russell Westbrook were Oklahoma City's star players. James played well, but the team didn't have room to give him the playing time he thought he deserved. After the 2011–2012 season, the Thunder traded James to the Houston Rockets.

The Rockets made James the focus of their team. He played more than he had with the Thunder, and he scored more too. With Oklahoma City, he had never scored more than 16.8 points per game in a season. In his first year in Houston, he put up 25.9 points per game. That was the fifth-best average in the NBA. He also led the league in free throw attempts.

James was grateful for his time with the Thunder. After he was traded, he posted this tweet: "I would love to thank Oklahoma City for 3 amazing years!"

James became a star in Houston, in part because of his long beard.

James glides to the hoop during a game against the Los Angeles Lakers in 2015.

In 2013–2014, James finished fifth in the NBA again with 25.4 points per game. The next season, he was named to the NBA All-Star Game for the third time in a row. James has become one of the best players in the NBA. But he still isn't satisfied. "I've got a long way to go, a lot of learning to do, improvements to make," he said. His desire to get better has helped make James one of the best basketball players in the world.

# Selected Career Highlights

**2014–2015**   Voted to the NBA All-Star Game for the third time

**2013–2014**   Voted to the NBA All-Star Game for the second time
Averaged 25.4 points per game with Houston
Finished third in the NBA with 665 free throw attempts

**2012–2013**   Traded from Oklahoma City to Houston before the start of the season
Voted to the NBA All-Star Game for the first time
Averaged 25.9 points per game with Houston
Led the NBA with 792 free throw attempts

**2011–2012**   Averaged 16.8 points per game with Oklahoma City
Helped Team USA win a gold medal at the Olympic Games in London

**2010–2011**   Averaged 12.2 points per game with Oklahoma City

**2009–2010**   Chosen by Oklahoma City with the third pick in the NBA draft
Averaged 9.9 points per game with Oklahoma City

**2008–2009**   Averaged 20.1 points per game with ASU
Led the conference with 270 free throw attempts

**2007–2008**   Averaged 17.8 points per game with ASU
Finished second in the conference with 224 free throw attempts

**2006–2007**   Averaged 18.8 points per game and shot 238 free throws with Artesia
Helped Artesia win the state championship

**2005–2006**   Averaged 18.8 points per game and shot 92 free throws with Artesia
Helped Artesia win the state championship

**2004–2005**   Averaged 13.2 points per game and shot 53 free throws with Artesia

**2003–2004**   Made the Artesia High School varsity team as a freshman

# Glossary

**alley-oops:** passes caught by a player in the air who tries to dunk the basketball before landing

**assist:** a pass to a teammate that helps the teammate score

**asthma:** a health problem that makes it hard to breathe

**career:** a job that someone does for a long time

**diploma:** a piece of paper that shows someone has graduated from a school

**draft:** a yearly event in which teams take turns choosing new players from a group

**dribble:** advance the ball by bouncing it

**drive:** move quickly to the basket with the ball

**Eastern Conference:** a group of NBA teams that play against one another. Eastern Conference teams include the Boston Celtics and Cleveland Cavaliers, among others.

**forward:** a player on a basketball team who usually plays close to the basket

**foul:** to hit or push another player in a way that is against the rules. A player who is fouled often gets to shoot free throws.

**free throws:** shots taken from behind the foul line on a basketball court

**guard:** a player on a basketball team who usually plays away from the basket

**layup:** a shot taken with one hand close to the basket

**rebounds:** plays where the ball is grabbed after a missed shot

**scouts:** basketball experts who watch players closely to judge their abilities

**steals:** plays that take possession of the ball from the other team

**three-point shot:** a shot taken from behind the three-point line on a basketball court

**varsity:** the top team at a school

**Western Conference:** a group of NBA teams that play against one another. Western Conference teams include the Oklahoma City Thunder and Houston Rockets, among others.

# Further Reading & Websites

Fishman, Jon M. *Kevin Love*. Minneapolis: Lerner Publications, 2014.

Gitlin, Marty. *Playing Pro Basketball*. Minneapolis: Lerner Publications, 2015.

Kennedy, Mike, and Mark Stewart. *Swish: The Quest for Basketball's Perfect Shot*. Minneapolis: Millbrook Press, 2009.

Savage, Jeff. *Kevin Durant*. Minneapolis: Lerner Publications, 2012.

NBA
http://www.nba.com
The NBA's official website provides fans with recent news stories, statistics, biographies of players and coaches, and information about games.

*Sports Illustrated Kids*
http://www.sikids.com
The *Sports Illustrated Kids* website covers all sports, including basketball.

LERNER
SOURCE

Expand learning beyond the printed book. Download free, complementary educational resources for this book from our website, www.lerneresource.com.

# Index

# Photo Acknowledgments

The images in this book are used with the permission of: AP Photo/Kathy Willens, pp. 4, 5, 6; AP Photo/Frank Franklin II, p. 7; © iStockphoto.com/ David Sucsy, p. 9; © Kevork Djansezian/Getty Images, p. 10; AP Photo/ Jim Mone, p. 12; © Bob Leverone/Sporting News/Getty Images, pp. 13, 15, 16; Jesse Beals/Icon SMI/Newscom, p. 14; Louis Lopez/Cal Sport Media/ Newscom, pp. 18, 19; Chris Coduto/Icon SMI 006/Newscom, p. 20; AP Photo/ Rich Pedroncelli, p. 21; AP Photo/Nati Harnik, p. 23; AP Photo/Jason DeCrow, p. 24; Boyd Ivey/Icon SMI/Newscom, p. 25; Jeff Haynes/Reuters/Newscom, p. 26; AP Photo/David J. Phillip, p. 27; AP Photo/Mark J. Terrill, p. 28; AP Photo/ Danny Johnston, p. 29.

Front cover: Tory Taormina/USA Today Sports/Newscom.

Main body text set in Caecilia LT Std 55 Roman 16/28.
Typeface provided by Adobe Systems.